Apollo Album

T0086632

for VIOLIN DUET
WITH PIANO ACCOMPANIMENT

by HARVEY S. WHISTLER and HERMAN A. HUMMEL

CONTENTS

RUBANK®

HAL•LEONARD®
CORPORATION
7777 W. BLUEMOUND RD. P.O. BOX 13819 MILWAUKEE, WI 53213

Evening Song
(Abendlied)

Piano Accompaniment

SCHUMANN

2

2 Country Dance
(Landlicher Tanz)

Piano Accompaniment

BEETHOVEN

3 String Salutation

Piano Accompaniment

SEITZ

Happy Holiday

Piano Accompaniment

BÖHM

5   Vienna Life

Piano Accompaniment

STRAUSS

Cielito Lindo

6

Piano Accompaniment

C. FERNANDEZ

Espressivo (Expressively)

7 Gaily the Troubadour

Piano Accompaniment

T. H. BAYLY

Con anima (With animation)

8   Waltz from H. M. S. Pinafore

Piano Accompaniment

SULLIVAN

9   Melody for Strings

Piano Accompaniment

RUBINSTEIN

10

Dream of Love
(Liebesträum)

Piano Accompaniment

LISZT

Jesu, Joy of Man's Desiring

Piano Accompaniment

BACH

12   It Came Upon the Midnight Clear

Piano Accompaniment

R. S. WILLIS

13   Andante from Iphigenia in Tauris

Piano Accompaniment

GLUCK

Ave Verum

14

Piano Accompaniment

MOZART

15 Silent Night

Piano Accompaniment

FRANK GRUBER

Apollo Album

for VIOLIN DUET
WITH PIANO ACCOMPANIMENT

by HARVEY S. WHISTLER
and HERMAN A. HUMMEL

HAL•LEONARD®
CORPORATION
7777 W. BLUEMOUND RD. P.O. BOX 13819 MILWAUKEE, WI 53213

PUBLISHED FOR:

First Violin (First Position)
Second Violin (First Position)
Piano Accompaniment

Apollo Album

for VIOLIN DUET
WITH PIANO ACCOMPANIMENT

by HARVEY S. WHISTLER and HERMAN A. HUMMEL

CONTENTS

RUBANK®

HAL•LEONARD® CORPORATION
7777 W. BLUEMOUND RD. P.O. BOX 13819 MILWAUKEE, WI 53213

Evening Song
(Abendlied)

1st Violin

SCHUMANN

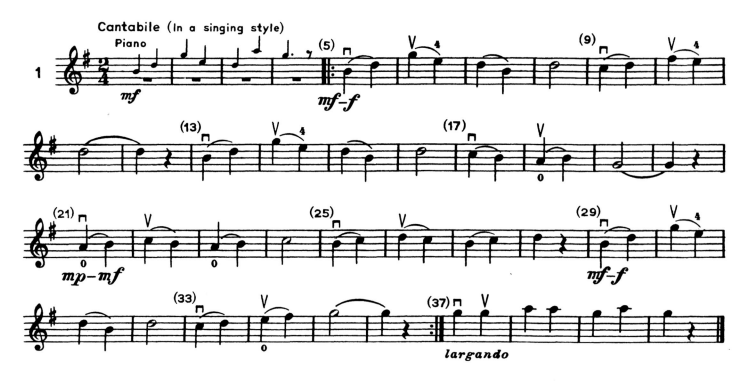

Country Dance
(Landlicher Tanz)

BEETHOVEN

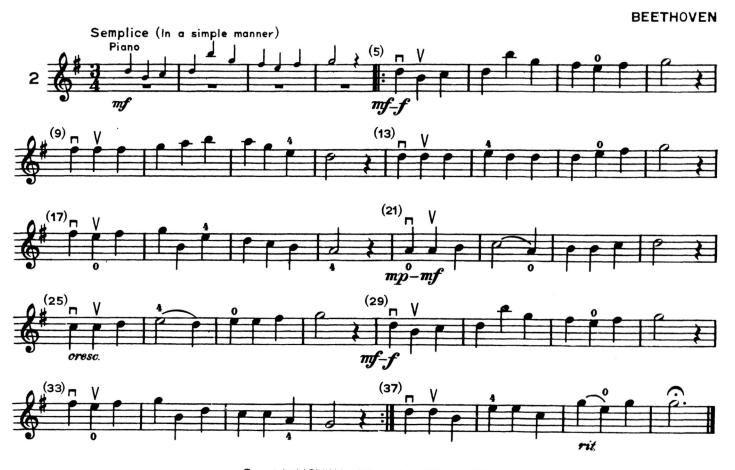

String Salutation

1st Violin

SEITZ

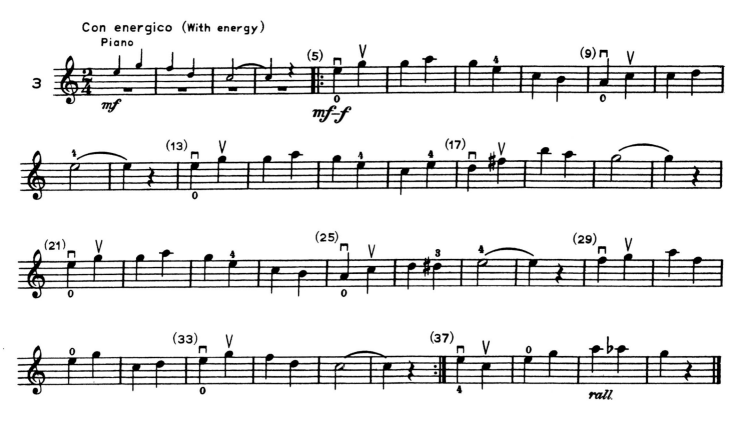

Happy Holiday

BÖHM

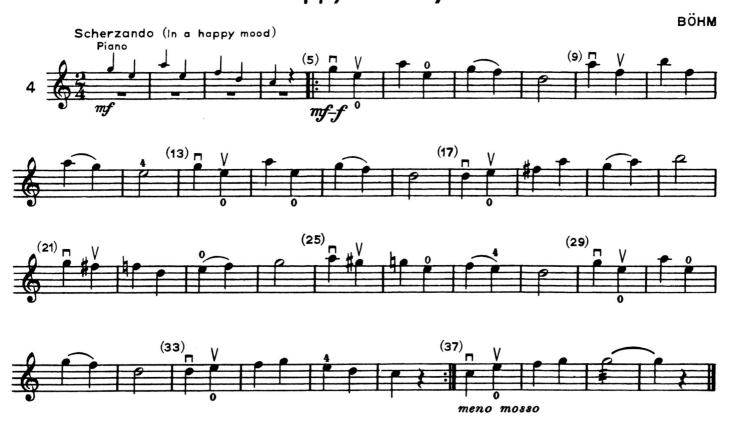

Vienna Life

1st Violin

STRAUSS

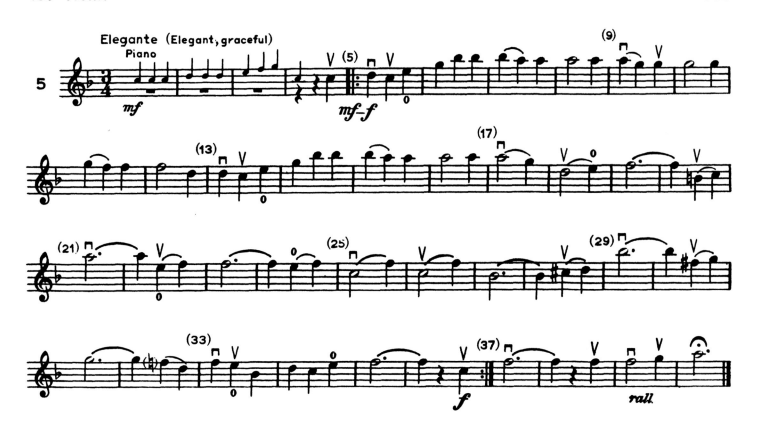

Cielito Lindo

C. FERNANDEZ

Rubank, Inc., Chicago, Ill.

Gaily the Troubadour

1st Violin

T. H. BAYLY

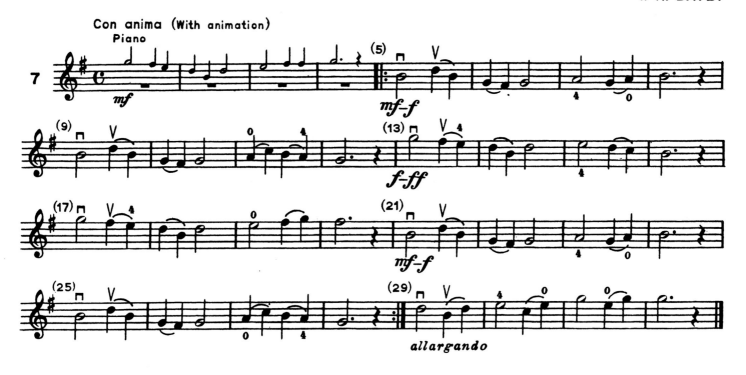

Waltz from H. M. S. Pinafore

SULLIVAN

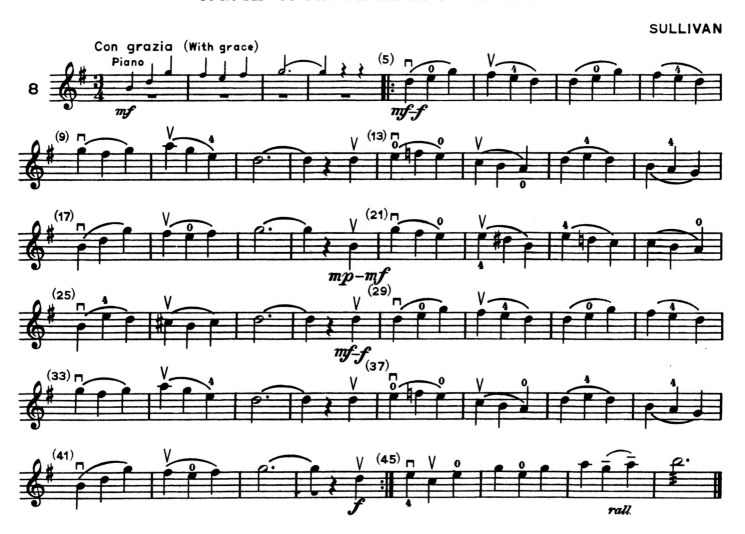

Melody for Strings

1st Violin

RUBINSTEIN

Con amore (With affection)

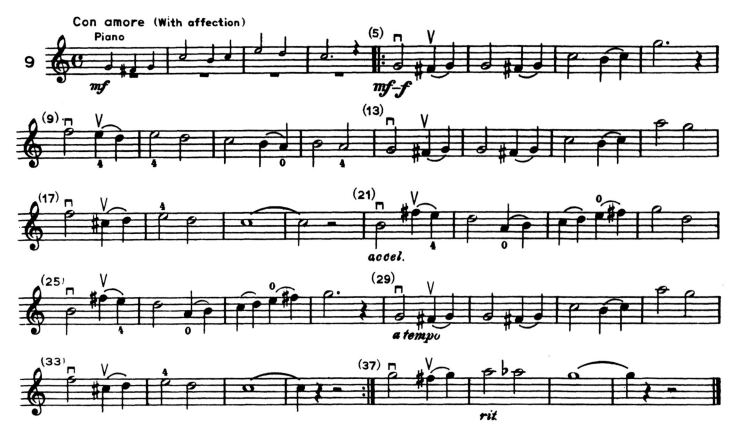

Dream of Love
(Liebesträum)

LISZT

Dolce (Sweetly)

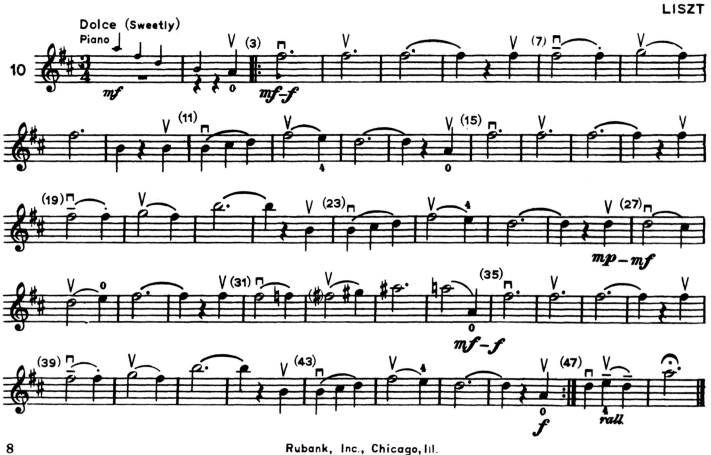

Rubank, Inc., Chicago, Ill.

Jesu, Joy of Man's Desiring

1st Violin

BACH

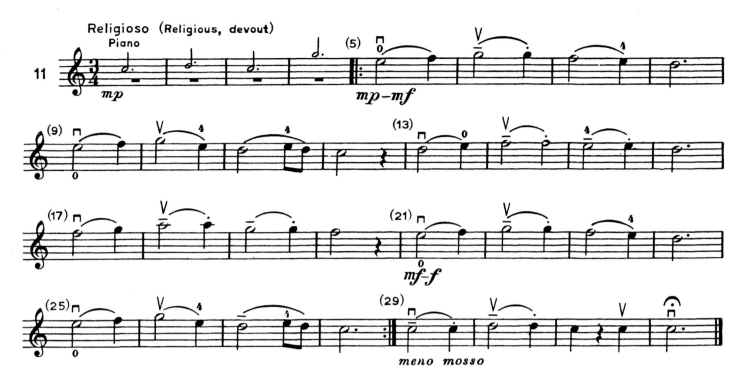

It Came Upon the Midnight Clear

R. S. WILLIS

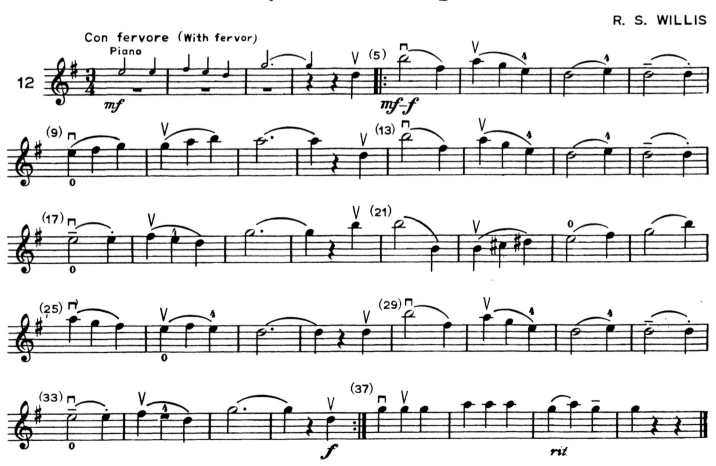

Andante from Iphigenia in Tauris

GLUCK

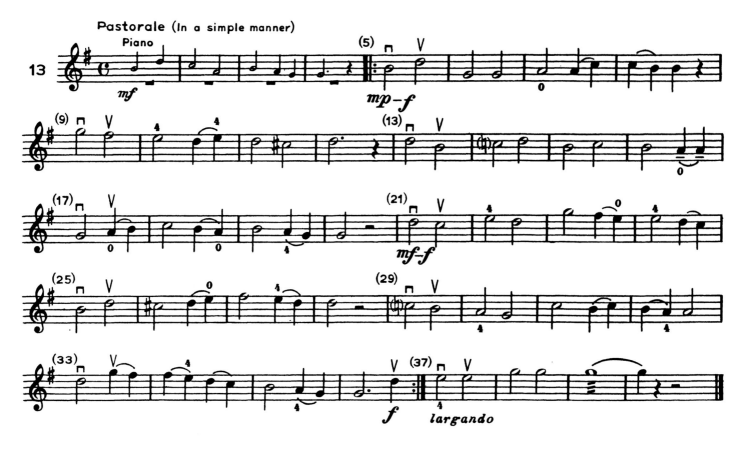

Ave Verum

MOZART

Rubank, Inc., Chicago, Ill

Silent Night

1st Violin

FRANZ GRUBER

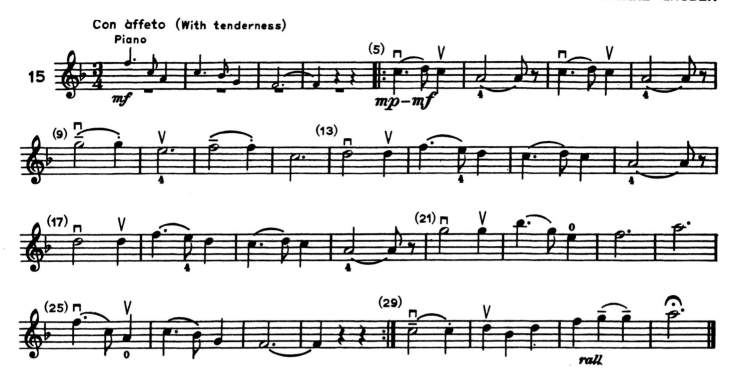

Drink To Me Only With Thine Eyes

Old English Ballad

Men of Harlech

Welsh Air

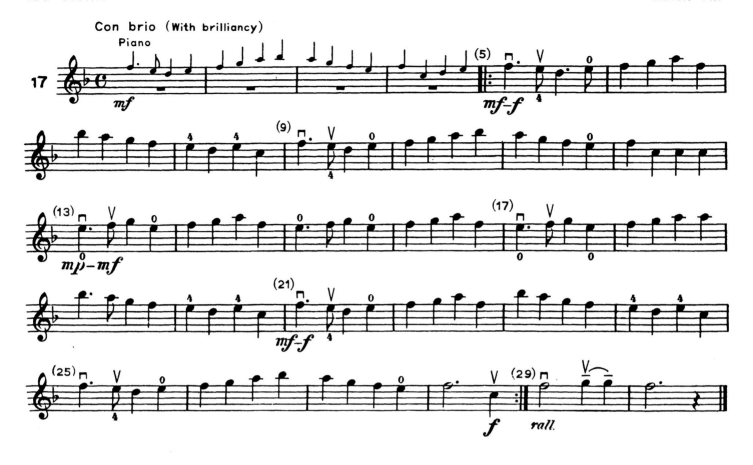

Alma Mater

School Song

Rubank, Inc., Chicago, Ill.

III.

Theme from First Symphony

1st Violin

BRAHMS

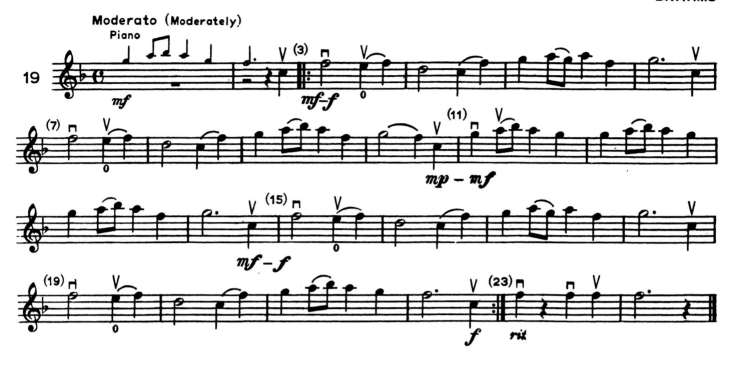

Excerpts from New World Symphony

DVORAK

Volga Boatman

1st Violin

Russian Folk Song

Con dolore (With grief)

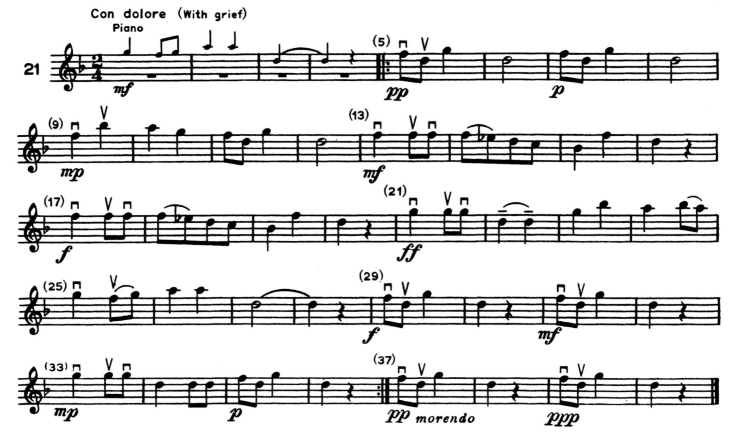

Jolly Coppersmith

PETERS

Allegro (Lively, quick)

Rubank, Inc., Chicago, III.

Oh! Promise Me

DE KOVEN

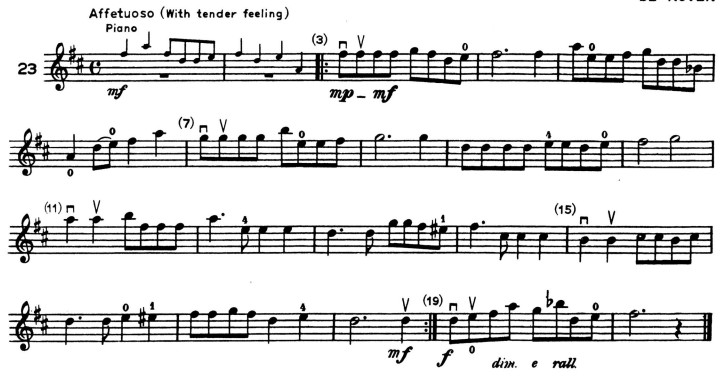

Rainbow Theme from Fantasie-Impromptu

CHOPIN

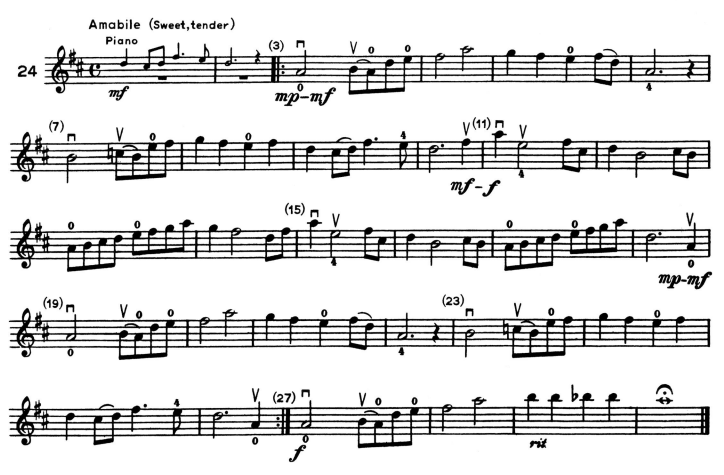

Chanson Triste

1st Violin

TSCHAIKOWSKY

Menuet from Symphony No. 7

HAYDN

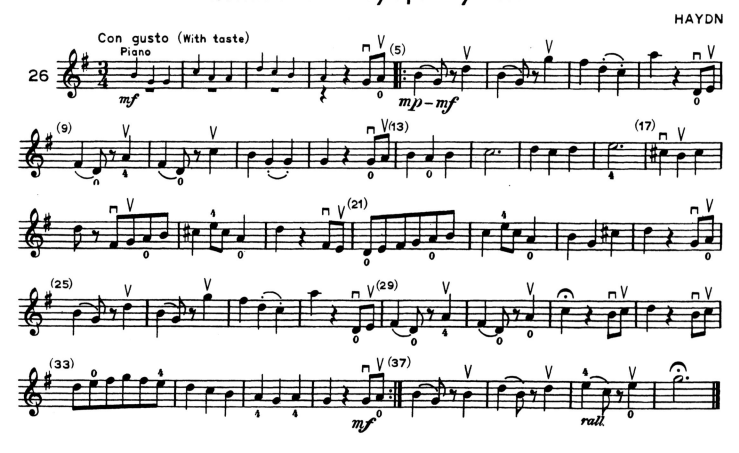

Rubank, Inc., Chicago, Ill

Rondo from Sonata, Op. 137, No. 1

1st Violin

Carnival of Venice

Italian Folk Song

Allegro from Der Freischutz

1st Violin

WEBER

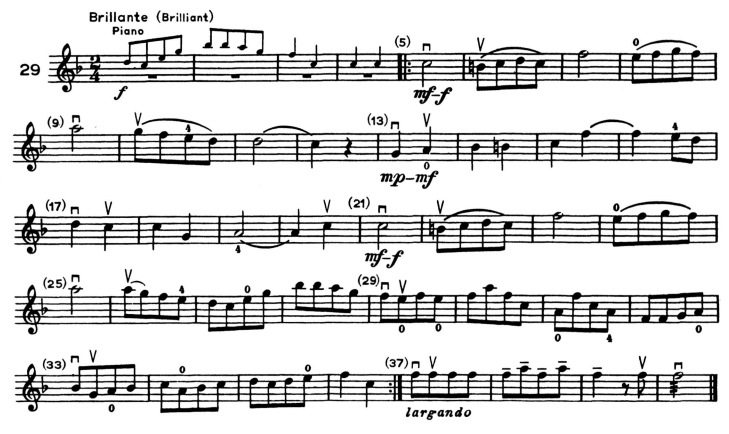

Processional Prelude

HANDEL

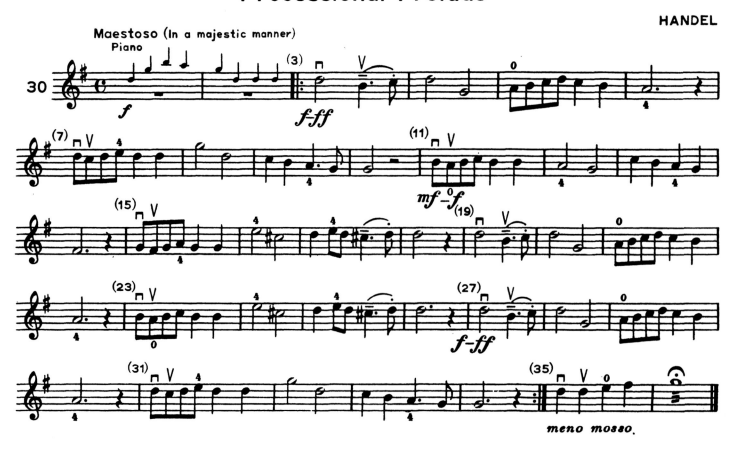

Rubank, Inc., Chicago, Ill.

Apollo Album

for VIOLIN DUET

WITH PIANO ACCOMPANIMENT

by HARVEY S. WHISTLER
and HERMAN A. HUMMEL

RUBANK®

HAL•LEONARD®
CORPORATION
7777 W. BLUEMOUND RD. P.O. BOX 13819 MILWAUKEE, WI 53213

PUBLISHED FOR:
First Violin (First Position)
Second Violin (First Position)
Piano Accompaniment

Apollo Album

for VIOLIN DUET
WITH PIANO ACCOMPANIMENT

by HARVEY S. WHISTLER and HERMAN A. HUMMEL

C O N T E N T S

RUBANK®

HAL•LEONARD CORPORATION
7777 W. BLUEMOUND RD. P.O. BOX 13819 MILWAUKEE, WI 53213

Evening Song
(Abendlied)

2nd Violin

SCHUMANN

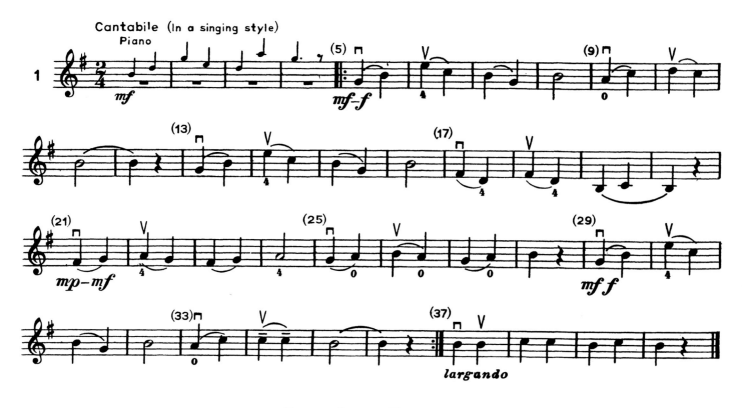

Country Dance
(Landlicher Tanz)

BEETHOVEN

String Salutation

2nd Violin

SEITZ

3

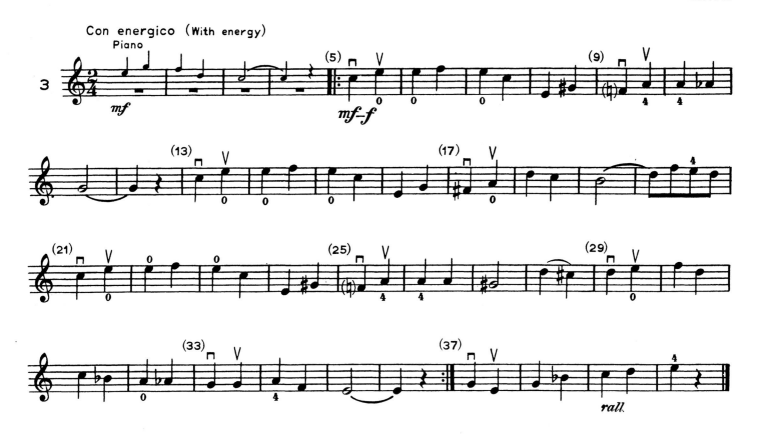

Happy Holiday

BÖHM

4

Vienna Life

STRAUSS

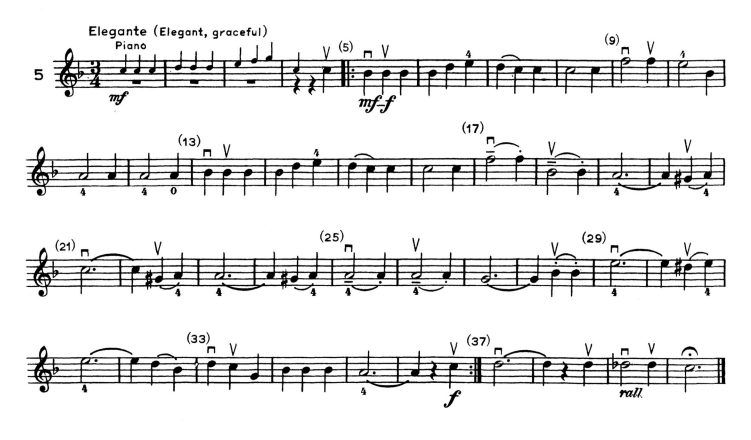

Cielito Lindo

C. FERNANDEZ

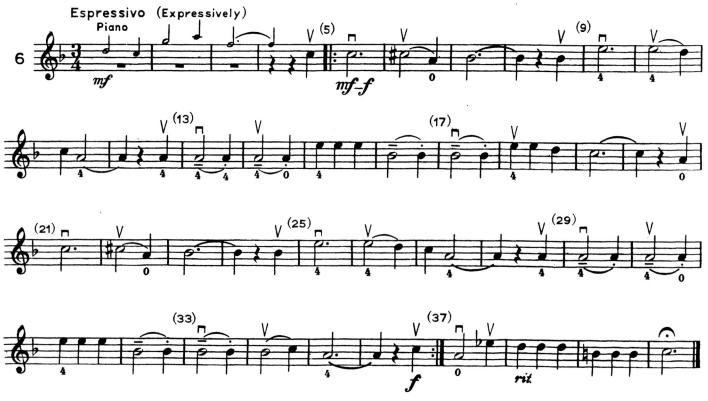

Rubank, Inc., Chicago, Ill.

Gaily the Troubadour

2nd Violin

T. H. BAYLY

Waltz from H. M. S. Pinafore

SULLIVAN

Melody for Strings

2nd Violin RUBINSTEIN

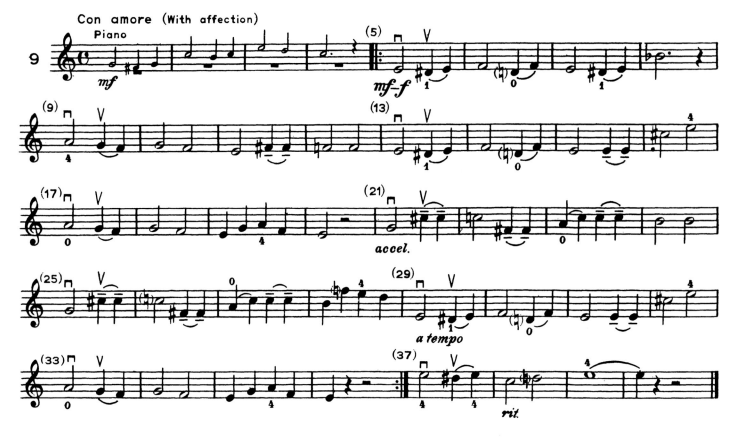

Dream of Love
(Liebesträum)

LISZT

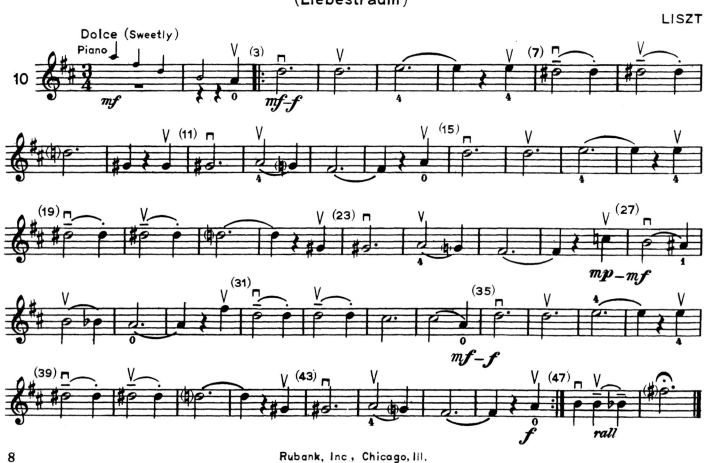

Rubank, Inc., Chicago, Ill.

Jesu, Joy of Man's Desiring

2nd Violin

BACH

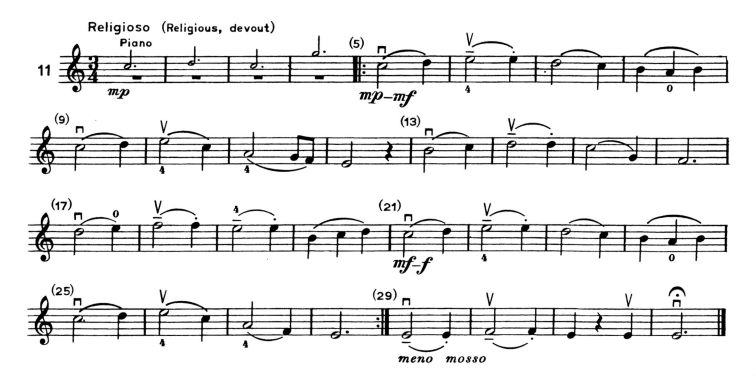

It Came Upon the Midnight Clear

R. S. WILLIS

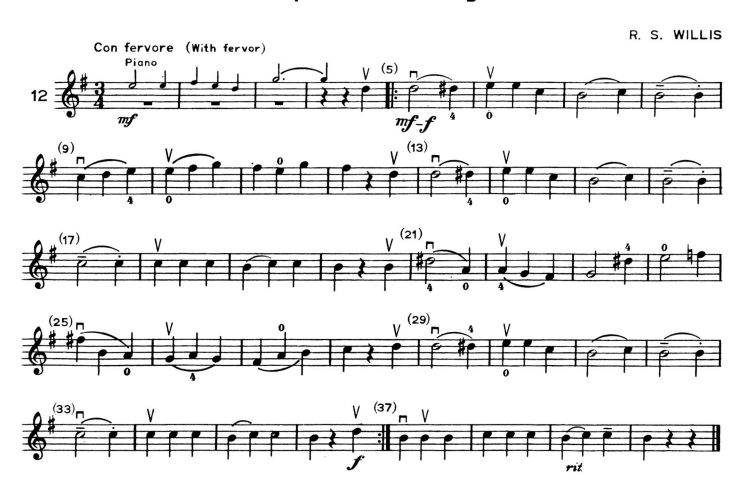

Andante from Iphigenia In Tauris

2nd Violin

GLUCK

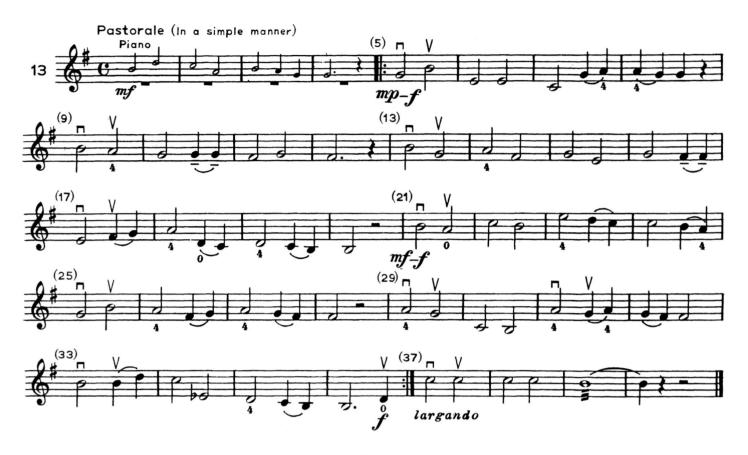

Ave Verum

MOZART

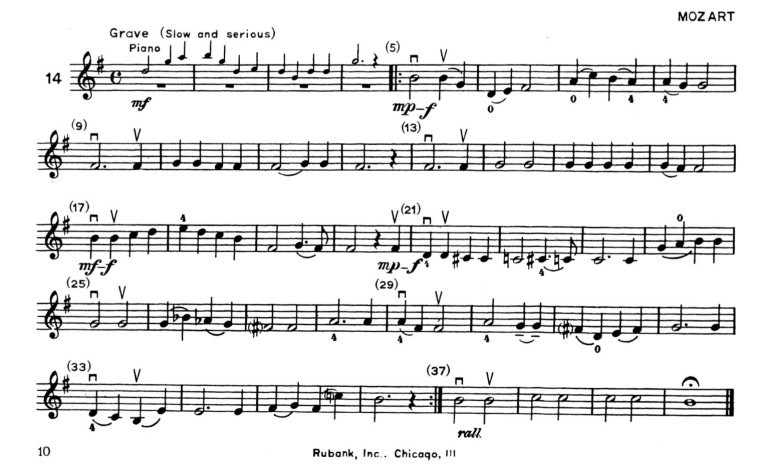

Rubank, Inc.. Chicago, III

Silent Night

FRANZ GRUBER

2nd Violin

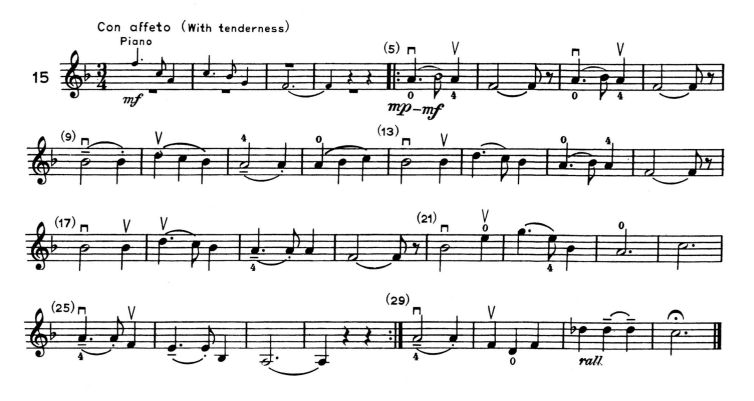

Drink to Me Only With Thine Eyes

Old English Ballad

Men of Harlech

2nd Violin

Welsh Air

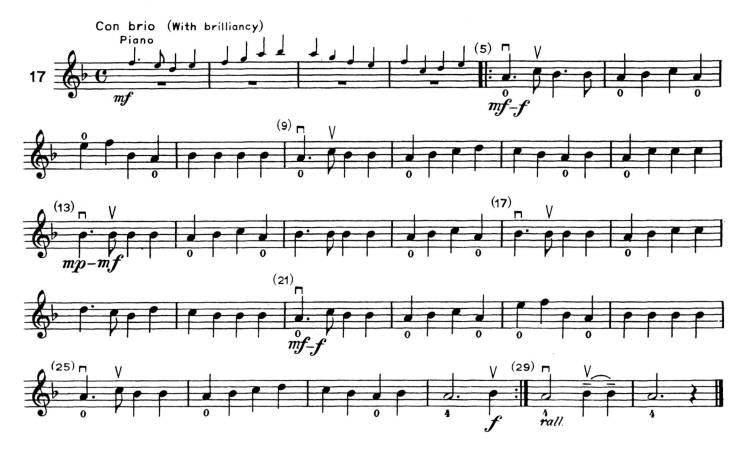

Alma Mater

School Song

Rubank, Inc., Chicago. Ill.

Theme from First Symphony

2nd Violin

BRAHMS

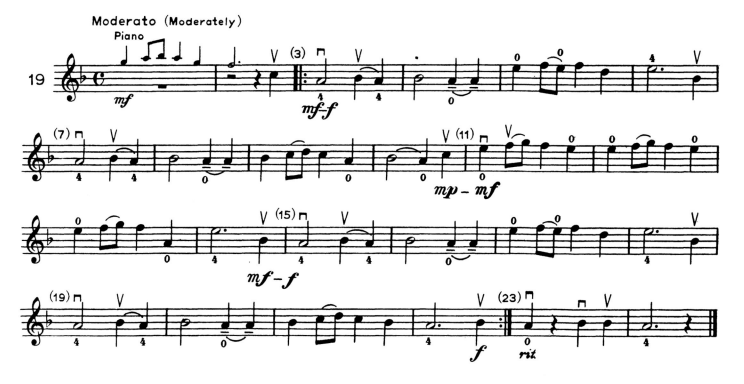

Excerpts from New World Symphony

DVORAK

Volga Boatman

Russian Folk Song

Jolly Coppersmith

PETERS

Rubank, Inc., Chicago, Ill.

Oh! Promise Me

DE KOVEN

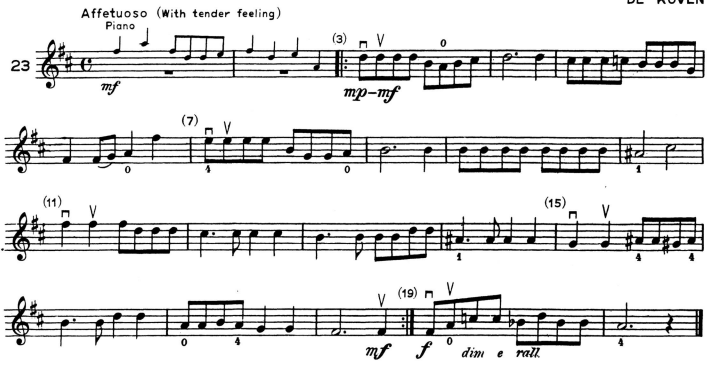

Rainbow Theme from Fantasie-Impromptu

CHOPIN

Rubank, Inc., Chicago, Ill.

Chanson Triste

2nd Violin

TSCHAIKOWSKY

Commodo (In a quiet manner)

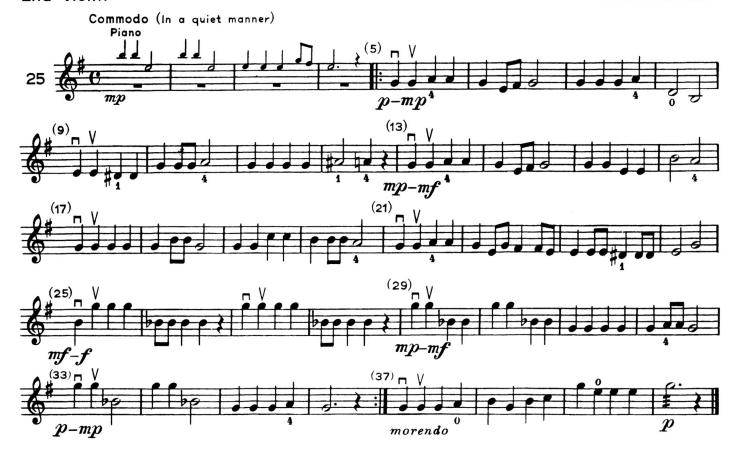

Menuet from Symphony No. 7

HAYDN

Con gusto (With taste)

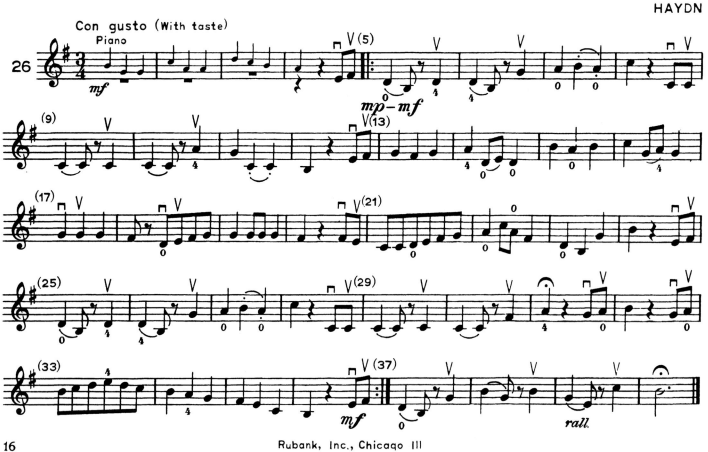

Rubank, Inc., Chicago Ill

Rondo from Sonata, Op. 137, No. 1

2nd Violin

SCHUBERT

Carnival of Venice

Italian Folk Song

Allegro from Der Freischutz

2nd Violin

WEBER

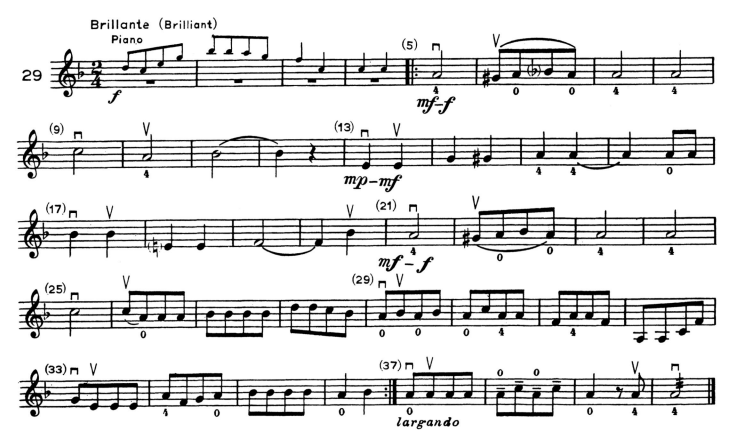

Processional Prelude

HANDEL

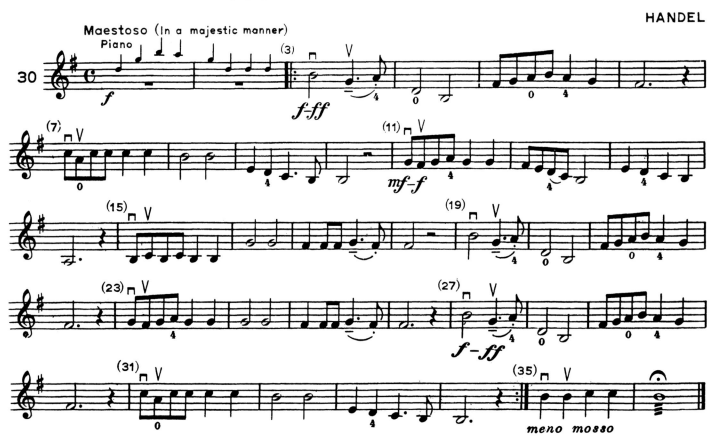

Rubank, Inc., Chicago, Ill.

Drink To Me Only With Thine Eyes

Piano Accompaniment

Old English Ballad

Men of Harlech

Piano Accompaniment

Welsh Air

Con brio (With brilliancy)

Alma Mater

Piano Accompaniment

19   # Theme from First Symphony

Piano Accompaniment

BRAHMS

Excerpts from New World Symphony

Piano Accompaniment

DVORAK

Larghetto (Moderately slow)

Volga Boatman

Piano Accompaniment

Russian Folk Song

Jolly Coppersmith

Piano Accompaniment

PETERS

Oh! Promise Me

Piano Accompaniment

DE KOVEN

Affetuoso (With tender feeling)

Rainbow Theme from Fantasie-Impromptu

Piano Accompaniment

CHOPIN

Chanson Triste

Piano Accompaniment

TSCHAIKOWSKY

Menuet from Symphony No. 7

Piano Accompaniment

HAYDN

Rondo from Sonata, Op. 137, No. 1

Piano Accompaniment

SCHUBERT

28 Carnival of Venice

Piano Accompaniment

Italian Folk Song

29 Allegro from Der Freischutz

Piano Accompaniment

WEBER

Processional Prelude

Piano Accompaniment

HANDEL